The pride of dying rich
raises the loudest laugh in hell.
John W. Foster

Lord, make me to know mine end,
and the measure of my days, what it is;
that I may know how frail I am.
Psalms 39:4

The last enemy that shall be destroyed
is death.
1 Corinthians 15:26

We are not human beings having a spiritual
experience.
We are spiritual beings having a human
experience
Dr. Wayne W. Dyer

God does not play dice with the universe.
Albert Einstein

A preacher and an atheist walked down a beach,

Each trying to convert the other.

They weren't gaining much headway.

Soon the atheist spied an expensive watch on a rock.

He picked it up.

"Wow! Look at all the perfect gears, spinning in such precise harmony... I wonder who made it?"

The preacher saw his chance; *"NOBODY."*

Well, *here's to 'nobody'*

death.

For the last 35 years I have had the privilege of touching people with chiropractic, bringing happiness and health to many people. But as wonderful as this has been, it has also kept me in a bubble where I see good outcomes, smiling adults and happy babies. It's sort of delusional, although incredibly nice.

Suddenly cancer reaches its ugly jaws out from the shadows. It bites your family and it poisons you. The bubble's gone. I must face her death; a process I can't stop or even palliate with my 'magic' adjustments. For someone accustomed to fixing folks' problems, it is all the more painful.

Of course, we needn't look far to see others having bigger demons to slay, more painful beds to lie in, and fewer support people to aid in their ultimate transition.

I take some solace in the fact that she's a Christian; I thank God her soul is in great hands forever.

So this makes two things I never thought I'd do; write about death… and preach.

For Linda

With love

Please Lord, Don't Let Me Die Last

A Philosopher's Free Verse on Death

FOR INFORMATION CONTACT

stevekooyers @ yahoo . com

"Always go to other people's funerals, otherwise they won't come to yours."
Yogi Berra

Disclaimers

Nothing in this book is a substitute for medical advice.

Some quotations were pasted from free sites on the Internet. No attempt was made to verify accuracy; however, due to the many sources citing the quotations it is likely that they are reasonably accurate. Other quotations were recalled from author's life experience. Further, all parables, allegories and metaphors are intended to convey *INTENT* over CONTENT. So if my CONTENT is incorrect or offensive, I apologize. Still, I hope you get my intent.

You might find diverse, contradictory and probably unsavory quotes, both Christian and non-Christian. This is not intended to cause denominational friction. It's just that death is democratic, so for once I shall be democratic, too.

My intent is to offer a sliver of philosophy, hoping it might support and put at ease those who are going through death's door before the rest of us go through it.

I never thought I'd write about death, but my sister Linda is rapidly approaching it at the time of this writing. Her courage has inspired me as much as her love has. And so it is that a doctor of life now writes on

CHAPTER ONE
POEMS ON DEATH AND DYING.

Death is obviously universal. Every one of us must experience it sooner or later. Just as there are many diverse circumstances surrounding birth, so it is with death. In the next few pages I'll cite a few situations that have singed my heart... and probably yours too.

There are two ways to view death. Some see it as the end. For them, it's lights out and that's all there is to it. I have always felt sorry for these people.

For others, including myself, death is an important transition. We believe there is an afterlife, and depending upon which belief system a person has, the various distinctions of each faith, sect and denomination hold special merit. I try not to split hairs... There isn't time for it.

The following poems are my original work.
I hope they give you strength.

Who has *Who?*

I have cancer.
It *does not* have me

Soon it will take my life
But it won't take *me*

They say I'm going to die
But have I really lived?

Have I done what I came here for?
Have I given the world my gift?

I will leave my people behind
Some of them for a long time
Others not so long
For tomorrow is promised to no one

There are worse things than dying
Like dying without Christ
Or before life's begun
Or the death of a daughter or son

I'm glad I'll go before the rest
It would hurt too much seeing the deaths of my best
All that remains is the end game
And I hope to play that with pride

To share my love and try not to hide
My feelings, hopes and mostly my love
For that's all I can leave behind
And all I can take with me above

Amen

This poem is shaped like a child's top spinning on the floor because all things revolve, recycle, renew. Everything comes around eventually. What better symbol than a child's top?

Revolution

My flesh is not me

Cancer may kill my car but not the driver

Disease may crash my plane, but not the pilot

Tumors may wreck the vessel, but never the wine

I am IN my body, but I am *not* my body

Soon my car will quit running;

I'll get out and shop

For a better

car.
Amen.Amen.Amen.Amen.Amen.Amen.Amen.AmenAmen

It's Not Me

They say I am dying, but they're wrong.

The only thing that's dying is my body.

I might be giving in, but I will never give up.

Medicine has tried and failed; I'm the proof.

Medicine is limited. God is not.

Some great doctors really tried to save me.

But saving and healing are two different things,

Just as the physical and spiritual bodies.

Sadly, most doctors don't accept this.

I see it in their eyes; they fear death

because they think death is the end.

It isn't.

Hallelujah!

Check-Out Time

It won't be long now, they tell me.

All the treatments and potions have failed

They say; *"It's in God's hands now."*

Actually, it was in God's hands all along.

My body's dying because doctors failed

I might be bitter, If only I had the time for it

Time is precious

Talk's cheap

Only

Love lasts

The Pain

My child is dying

All I can feel is pain

Now I know how God felt

When we killed his son

Later I might feel the joy

God felt when Jesus rose again.

But now all I have is anger and pain.

I'm a short-sighted mortal, Lord.

Please forgive me for that.

Amen.

An Act of God

I lost a loved one
to a drunk driver

My soul is ripped apart.
To think of that bloody crash

On some dirty piece of highway...
Makes me long for revenge.

I know it's wrong, Lord,
But I can't help but hate.

I know it takes time, too
But that doesn't help

Right now,
Your Plan sucks

Forgive me, Lord...

All I feel
is pain.

The 'Old' Patient

I used to be somebody.
Now I am just a gown, a chart
And a beating heart

My life has shrunk down
to a white room and Black Death.
And schedules...

They even gave me
a schedule for dying.
I hope not to keep it

But hope is for the living,
Not for me.
I'm checking out.

All I have left is faith...
It's shaky, but it's still here,
Praise God.

When my family comes
And sees this empty bed
They will grieve. Then
They'll see that
I am risen
Amen

My baby died

My baby died.
Is there a worse feeling?
If so, I hope you never feel it.

A life is over, before it started
How sick is that?

Adults get time to prove
Themselves worthy or not.
Usually it's the latter.

But my baby never had the chance
Life isn't fair.
This proves it

But earthly life is one thing
Heavenly life is another.
God has special love
For babies

Hallelujah!

Please, Lord, Don't Let Me Die Last

Nobody wants to die.
But everyone wants to go to Heaven.
I am no different.

And now it's my time
To face life's final challenge
I am wracked with fear.

Soothing words don't help.
Platitudes are water off a duck's back
Worldly matters fade off the charts

But of it all, I take solace in one thing
At least I won't die last.
I couldn't bear outliving my family,
Watching them die one by one
Going to funeral after funeral
Each one ripping a new hole in my soul.

So Lord, take my soul while it's intact.
It's selfish I know, but forgive me.
And, please Lord…
Don't let me die last.

Amen

They Still Don't Get It

It won't be long now.
I have made my peace with it...

Soon I will pass to the next life
as we all must

Those who I leave behind
are struggling with it

They squabble over terms
and assets and memorabilia

They still don't get it...
It's not about stuff or politics
or agendas

I wish I could open their eyes
Before closing mine.

Dear God, forgive them...
And me.

Amen

CHAPTER TWO
FAMOUS QUOTES ON DYING

The trouble with quotes about death is that 99.999 percent of them are made by people who are still alive
Josh Bruns

And fear not them which kill the body, but are not able to kill the soul: but rather fear him which is able to destroy both soul and body in hell.
Matthew 10:28

"You better enjoy livin' baby,
'cause dying is a pain in the ass"
- Frank Sinatra (1915-1998)

At death we cross from one territory to another, but we'll have no trouble with visas. Our representative is already there, preparing for our arrival. As citizens of heaven, our entrance is incontestable.
Erwin Lutzer

Because I could not stop for death, He kindly stopped for me; The carriage held but just ourselves and immortality.
Emily Dickinson

But learn that to die is a debt we must all pay.
Euripides

Come he slow or come he fast.
It is but death who comes at last.
Sir Walter Scott

Death -- the last sleep?
No, it is the final awakening.
Sir Walter Scott

Death is an endless night so awful to contemplate that it can make us love life and value it with such passion that it may be
the ultimate cause of all joy and all art.
Paul Theroux

Death is as sure for that which is born,
as birth is for that which is dead.
Therefore grieve not for what is inevitable.
Bhagavad Gita

Death is the liberator of him whom freedom cannot release, the physician of him whom medicine cannot cure, and the comforter of him
whom time cannot console.
Charles Caleb Colton

Death may be the greatest of all human blessings.
Socrates

Death may be the King of terrors...
but Jesus is the King of kings!
Dwight L. Moody

Death twitches my ear.
"Live," he says, "I am coming."
Virgil

Death was afraid of him because
he had the heart of a lion.
Arabian Proverb

Die when I may, I want it said of me
by those who knew me best,
that I always plucked a thistle and planted a flower
where I thought a flower would grow.
Abraham Lincoln

Every man must do two things alone;
he must do his own believing
and his own dying.
Martin Luther

Fear of death has been the greatest ally
of tyranny past and present.
Sydney Hook

Fish die belly upward, and rise to the surface.
Its their way of falling.
Andre Gide

For 'Tis not in mere death that men die most.
Elizabeth Barrett Browning

For we brought nothing into this world,
and it is certain we can carry nothing out.
1 Timothy 6:7

God's retirement plan is out of this world
Anonymous

Good God! how often are we to die
before we go quite off this stage?
In every friend we lose a part of ourselves,
and the best part.
Alexander Pope

Good men must die, but death cannot kill their names.
Proverb

He has gone over to the majority.
Petronius

He who can no longer pause to wonder and stand
rapt in awe is as good as dead; his eyes are closed.
Albert Einstein

He whom the Gods love dies young,
while he is in health, has his senses
and his judgments sound.
Titus Maccius Plautus

How strange this fear of death is!
We are never frightened at a sunset.
George Macdonald

I am ready to meet God face to face tonight
and look into those eyes of infinite holiness,
for all my sins are covered
by the atoning blood.
R. A. Torrey

I care not, a man can die but once;
we owe God and death.
William Shakespeare

I died a mineral, and became a plant.
I died a plant and rose an animal.
I died an animal and I was man.
Why should I fear?
When was I less by dying?
Jalal-Uddin Rumi

I hate funerals and would not attend my own if it could be avoided, but it is well for every man to stop once in a while to think of what sort of a collection of mourners he is training for his final event.
Robert T. Morris

I have a piece of great and sad news to tell you:
I am dead.
Jean Cocteau

I have lived, and I have run the course which fortune allotted me; and now my shade shall descend illustrious to the grave.
Virgil

I look upon death to be as necessary to our constitution as sleep. We shall rise refreshed in the morning.
Benjamin Franklin

I look upon life as a gift from God. I did nothing to earn it. Now that the time is coming to give it back, I have no right to complain.
Joyce Cary

I shall not wholly die, and
a great part of me will escape the grave.
Horace

I will be conquered; I will not capitulate.
Samuel Johnson

I'm trying to die correctly,
but it's very difficult, you know.
Lawrence Durrell

I

If Nature denies eternity to beings, it follows that their destruction is one of her laws. Now, once we observe that destruction is so useful to her that she absolutely cannot dispense with it from this moment onward the idea of annihilation which we attach to death ceases to be real what we call the end of the living animal is no longer a true finish, but a simple transformation, a transmutation of matter. According to these irrefutable principles, death is hence no more than a change of form, an imperceptible passage from one existence into another.

Marquis De Sade

If some persons died, and others did not die,
death would be a terrible affliction.
Jean De La Bruyere

Ignore death up to the last moment; then,
when it can't be ignored any longer,
have yourself squirted full of morphia
and shuffle off in a coma.
Thoroughly sensible, humane
and scientific, eh?
Aldous Huxley

In the democracy of the dead all men at last are
equal. There is neither rank nor station nor
prerogative in the republic of the grave.
John J. Ingalls

In the long run we are all dead.
John Maynard Keynes

It is a sign of a creeping inner death
when we no longer can praise the living.
Eric Hoffer

Living is death; dying is life.
We are not what we appear to be.
On this side of the grave we are exiles, on that
citizens; on this side orphans, on that children;
Henry Ward Beecher

Lord, make me to know mine end,
and the measure of my days, what it is;
that I may know how frail I am.
Psalms 39:4

Oh you who have been removed from God
in his solitude by the abyss of time,
how can you expect to reach him without dying?
Hallaj

One should die proudly
when it is no longer possible to live proudly.
Friedrich Nietzsche

Perhaps the whole root of our trouble, the human trouble, is that we will sacrifice all the beauty of our lives, will imprison ourselves in totems, taboos, crosses, blood sacrifices, steeples, mosques, races, armies, flags, nations, in order to deny the fact of death, which is the only fact we have.
James Baldwin

Precious in the sight of the Lord
is the death of His godly ones.
Psalms 116:15

The Father is the Giver of Life;
but the Mother is the Giver of Death,
because her womb is the gate of ingress to matter,
and through her life is ensouled to form,
and no form can be either infinite or eternal.
Death is implicit in birth.
Kabbalah

The hour of departure has arrived
and we go our ways; I to die, and you to live.
Which is better? Only God knows.
Socrates

The last enemy that shall be destroyed is death.
1 Corinthians 15:26

The pride of dying rich raises the loudest laugh in hell.
John W. Foster

The white man's dead forget the country of their birth
when they go to walk among the stars.
Our dead never forget this beautiful earth,
for it is the mother of the red man.
Chief Seattle

There is a remedy for everything; it is called death.
Portuguese Proverb

Though it be in the power
of the weakest arm
to take away life,
it is not in the strongest
to deprive us of death.
Sir Thomas Browne

To a father, when a child dies, the future dies; to a
child when a parent dies, the past dies.
Red Auerbach

We are all dead men on leave.
Eugene Levine

We are not victims of aging, sickness and death.
These are part of scenery, not the seer, who is
immune to any form of change.
This seer is the spirit,
the expression of eternal being.
Deepak Chopra

We come and cry and that is life,
we cry and go and that is death.
Proverb

We should weep for men at their birth,
not at their death.
Charles De Montesquieu

We sometimes congratulate ourselves
at the moment of waking from a troubled dream;
it may be so, the moment after death.
Nathaniel Hawthorne

When the body sinks into death, the essence of man is revealed. Man is a knot, a web, a mesh into which relationships are tied. Only those relationships matter. The body is an old crock that nobody will miss. I have never known a man to think of himself when dying. Never.
Antoine De Saint-Exupery

While I thought that I was learning how to live,
I have been learning how to die.
Leonardo Da Vinci

Whoever has lived long enough to find out what life is,
knows how deep a debt of gratitude we owe to Adam,
the first great benefactor of our race.
He brought death into the world.
Mark Twain

There are only two forces in the world,
the sword and the spirit.
In the long run the sword will always
be conquered by the spirit.
Napoleon Bonaparte

Your lost friends are not dead, but gone before,
advanced a stage or two upon that road which you
must travel in the steps they trod.
Aristophanes

CHAPTER THREE
HUMOROUS QUOTES

I'm not afraid to die, I just don't want to be there
when it happens.
Woody Allen

A dead atheist is someone who is all dressed up
with no place to go.
James Duffecy

Always go to other people's funerals,
otherwise they won't come to yours.
Yogi Berra

Death is nature's way of saying, Your table's ready.
Robin Williams

For days after death hair and fingernails continue
to grow, but phone calls taper off.
Johnny Carson

I don't believe in an after life, although
I am bringing a change of underwear.
Woody Allen

Health nuts are going to feel stupid someday,
lying in hospitals dying of nothing.
Redd Foxx

I am dying beyond my means.
Oscar Wilde

Let us endeavor so to live that when we come to die
even the undertaker will be sorry.
Mark Twain

My idea of walking into the jaws of death is marrying some woman who has lost three husbands.
Kin Hubbard

I never wanted to see anybody die, but
there are a few obituary notices
I have read with pleasure.
Clarence Darrow

To stop sinning suddenly.
Elbert Hubbard

When I die I want to decompose in a barrel of porter and have it served in all the pubs in Dublin.
J. P. Donleavy

When I die, I want to go peacefully like my Grandfather did -- in his sleep. Not yelling and screaming like the passengers in his car.
Anonymous

You cannot live without lawyers, and certainly you cannot die without them.
Joseph H. Choate

“God is dead. Nietsche
Nietsche is dead. God”
anon

Union General John Sedgwick, when his men warned him to be wary of Confederate sharpshooters: "They couldn't hit an elephant at this dist..."

CHAPTER FOUR
JOKES

(Most of the following from Digg . com, basic quotes or other humor websites you can easily surf. Note; edited for brevity.)

The Mule

Once there was a woman married to an annoying man. He complained about everything. The mule got annoyed and kicked him.

At the funeral, when men walked by the wife she shook her head yes. When women walked by she shook her head no. The minister asked her why.

"The men said how sorry they felt for me and I was saying, 'Yes, I'll be alright.' The women walked by... asking if the mule is for sale. "

A Savant?

"Now my grandfather knew the exact day of the year he was going to die. Not only that, but he knew what time he would die, too!"

"Wow, that's Incredible. How did he know all of that?"

"A judge told him."

God bless Daddy

One night, a father overheard his son saying his prayers, "God bless Mommy, Daddy, and Grammy. Goodbye Grampa."

The next day, the Grandfather died.

About a month later, the father overheard his son's prayers again; "God bless Mommy and Daddy. Goodbye Grammy."

The next day, Grammy died.

Two weeks later, the father heard his son praying, "God bless Mommy. Goodbye Daddy." He got scared. The next morning, he got up early and went to work. He stayed in his office all day. Finally, after midnight, he went home... Alive! He crawled into bed and apologized; "I'm sorry honey, I had a really bad day."

"*You* had a bad day? That *nice mailman* dropped dead on the porch this morning!"

Careful!

A funeral service was held for a woman. The pallbearers are carrying the casket out, accidentally bumping into a wall. They hear a faint moan. They open the casket and find the woman alive. She lives for ten more years and then dies. At the end of the ceremony the pallbearers are again carrying the casket.

The husband cries out; *"Watch out for the wall!"*

What a way to go

An old preacher was dying. He sent a message for his doctor and his lawyer. As they entered his bedroom the preacher motioned to sit on each side of the bed. The preacher smiled and stared at the ceiling.

They were flattered that the preacher asked them to be with him during his final moments. They were also puzzled; he'd never indicated that he liked either of them. They recalled his long, uncomfortable sermons about greed, covetousness and avarice. Finally, the doctor asks, "Preacher, why did you ask the two of us to come?"

"Well, Jesus died between two thieves ... so that's how I want to go."

It's not our plan...

A stingy old lawyer had a terminal illness. He was determined to disprove the old saying, "You can't take it with you." So the old ambulance chaser finally figured out how to take some of his money with him.

He had his wife withdraw enough money to fill two pillowcases and put the bags in the attic, above his bed... When he passed, he would reach out and grab the bags on his way to heaven.

Several weeks after the funeral, the widow went to the attic and snatched the money. "Oh, that old fool; he should've had me put the money *in the basement."*

We've got plans

An elderly man lay dying in his bed, suddenly smelling his favorite; freshly baked chocolate chip cookies. He gathered his strength and struggled out of bed. With great effort he got down the stairs, gripping the railing with both hands. Trembling with weakness, he leaned against the doorframe, gazing into the kitchen.

On the kitchen table were hundreds of his favorite cookies. Was it a kind gesture from his wife? Mustering great final effort, he crawled to the table. He fought his way to a standing position; he reached shakily for a cookie when his wife hollered.

"HEY! Stay out of those! *They're for the funeral."*

An elderly couple was standing on the back of a cruise ship when a wave washed the husband overboard. They searched for days, so the captain sent the old woman to shore, promising to tell her if they found him.

Three weeks later she got a fax from the captain; "Sorry to say, we found your husband dead at the bottom of the ocean. Stuck to his butt was an oyster with a pearl worth $50,000. Please advise"

She faxed back: "Send me the pearl; re-bait the trap"

Mr. “Not so Right”

John: "I heard you got married again, Ken."
"Yes, for the fourth time."
"What happened to your first three wives?"
"They all died."
"Oh, that's terrible. How did they die?
"The first ate poisonous mushrooms."
"How awful! What about the second?"
"She ate poisonous mushrooms."
"Wow; and the third? Did she die from mushrooms?"
"Nope; broken neck."
"I see, an accident."
"Not exactly - she wouldn't eat her mushrooms."

A DYING ATHEIST

An 82 year-old atheist lay on his hospital bed, breathing his last. A chaplain entered his room.

“Sir, would you like me to pray with you?”
“No, thank you... I don't believe in God.”
“Well, if you change your mind, call me.”

With that, the chaplain left the man alone with his thoughts. Soon an angel entered his mind.
“John, would you like to accept God now?”
The astonished atheist couldn't believe it; there were actually ANGELS! Still, he had his earthful thinking.

“So *NOW* you appear! Where were you all those years... when I NEEDED YOU?”

The angel was chosen because she had patience.
“What... Didn't you get the *messages?”*
“HUH? What messages?”

“Let's see... By rough count, we sent you: the Bible, the Koran, the Kaballah... Christ, Allah, Buddha... sixteen church marquis you drove past on your way to work every day... two hundred fifty-two Jehovah's Witnesses knocked on your door... eighty-eight Mormon missionaries... You stayed in ninety-three hotels with Bibles placed by the Gideons... Sixty years of televangelists on four TV channels... Twelve major motion pictures... fifty chanting Hare Krishnas at airports... and still you managed to ignore all of them, including that nice chaplain that just left... what do you say to that?”

The old non-believer refused to be bullied.

“I'd say those messages came from MEN... and men can't be trusted... besides, I'm a man of science!”
The angel remained calm.
“Well how did you think God would send his messages, except through worthy people?”

“I only believe in things I can see, touch and prove.”

“Ok, let's work with that; your birth, the births of your three children... the earth and stars... countless random acts of kindness and tolerance... and love, John... all of these are signs of God's existence and love... What part don't you get?”

“Ah, balderdash! That's just... biological imperative.”
The angel began to depart, but took one more shot at his hell-bound spirit.

“Well, I don't know what else to say to convince you, except; 'trust in God. Delight thyself also in the...”
“I don't believe it.”
“I know you don't believe... that's why He sent me. Well if you change your mind, call us, but I wouldn't wait long... it's time to wake up and smell the RAPTURE.”

John woke from his 'dream', wondering....

“Could it be true?”

Then he died.

CHAPTER FIVE
CHOICE EPITAPHS
(some pasted from Digg, senior-site, etc)

Silver City, Nevada

Here lies a man named Zeke.

Second fastest draw in Cripple Creek.

Boot Hill Museum, Dodge City, Kansas

Here lies the body of Arkansas Jim.

We made the mistake, But the joke's on him.

Culver City

He called

Bill Smith

A Liar

Cripple Creek, CO

A woman who died in Colorado Springs. She had been married to a Texan who is buried in Texas.

I would

rather be here

than in Texas.

Here lies old Rastus Sominy

Died a-eating hominy

In 1859 anno domini

Savannah, Georgia

In a New Jersey cemetery

Rebecca Freeland

1741

She drank good ale,

good punch and wine

And lived to the age of 99.

Falkirk, England

Here lies Kelly,
We buried him today.
He lived the life of Riley,
....when Riley was away!

Here Lies The Body Of A Man Who Died
Nobody Mourned - Nobody Cried
How He Lived - How He Fared
Nobody Knows - Nobody Cared

Sacred to the memory of Jared Bates,
Who died Aug. the 6th, 1800.
His widow, aged 24, lives at 7 Elm Street,
Has every qualification for a good wife,
And longs to be comforted.

1690

Here lie the bones of Joseph Jones

Who ate while he was able.

But once overfed, he dropt down dead

And fell beneath the table.

When from the tomb, to meet his doom,

He arises amidst sinners.

Since he must dwell in heaven or hell,

Take him - whichever gives the best dinners.

On a lawyer in England:

Sir John Strange.

Here lies an honest lawyer.

And that is Strange.

Here lies the father of 29.

He would have had more

But he didn't have time.

Moultrie, Georgia

In a New Hampshire cemetery.

Tears cannot restore her --

-- therefore I weep.

Here lies

Elizabeth,

my wife for 47 years,

and this is the first damn thing

she ever done to oblige me.

Streatham, England

On the death of a watchmaker:

Here lies in horizontal position the outside case of Dear George Routleight, watchmaker, whose abilities in that line were an honor to his profession -- integrity was the mainspring, and prudence the regulator of all the actions of his life. Humane, generous, and liberal, his hand never stopped until he had relieved distress. So nicely regulated were all his movements that he never went wrong, except when set agoing by people who did not know his key; even then he was easily set right again. He had the art of disposing his time so well that the hours glided away in one continued round of pleasure and delight, till an unlucky moment put a period to his existence. He departed this life November 14, 1802, aged fifty-seven. Wound up in hopes of being taken in hand by his Maker and being thoroughly cleansed, repaired, and set agoing in the world to come. St Petrock's Church, Lyford, Devon, England

On an Auctioneer:

Jedediah Goodwin

Auctioneer

Born 1828

Going!

Going!!

Gone!!!

1876

CHAPTER SIX

NON-SCIENCE

(pronounced almost like 'nonsense')

A scientist kept bragging that he could create life; he had the gadgets for it. Finally, God showed, to challenge the mortal's simplistic arrogance; "Let's have a race to see who can create life first." The scientist says; *"GAME ON!"* He reaches down for a liter of earth to start his experiment.
God says; "Hey! *GET YOUR OWN DIRT."*

It should be obvious that a sentient being CREATED the universe. We call it god. Other cultures throughout history had their names for it... but one thing's clear; an intelligent force created it all.

A scientific axiom says:
"Matter can neither be created or destroyed."

Then they lay the "Big Bang" theory on us. One cannot "Bang" nothing and get anything, much less an infinite number of stars, planets, asteroids, meteors and space. The theory is impossible, by scientific definition.

We are left with two deductions; either the universe has ALWAYS been here or somebody made it. Now, I don't get 'always' or 'infinite'. I keep thinking 'there must've been a point in time, just before *'always'* started. There ought to be an end to *'infinite,'* too.

It's odd, how science lauds 'infinite,' yet denies god...
I still don't get it.

The Death Gene

Modern technology is beginning to catch up to the timeless concept that death is necessary.

Recently I watched a TV program on nicotine. One of the more surprising facts was that it causes cellular hyperplasia, which causes cancer.

Ironically, nicotine kills off the "Death Gene"... a genetic code that causes the cell to die at its predetermined age. So, without the genetic instruction to die, the cell lives too long; it keeps reproducing past its prime. The resulting replications are fertile soil for mutations; one being malignancy.

Imagine; approximately FOUR BILLION cells in your body; and every one of them is *programmed to die.* And what is the purpose? *LIFE.* The cell deaths allow for continued high quality life...

We are each of us born, material proof that our souls came from somewhere and are now temporarily housed in physical bodies. And yet, even as infants, our every cell already has its plan to die. It must follow that we also are programmed to die, to contribute our soul-spark to the continued health of the spiritual collective that most folks call God.

Whether or not you believe in God is *your business.* The death gene is already in place... but I'd say now's a good reason to start praying.

Science or God? Your choice.

I find it odd that those who do not study science are in awe of it, while those that study it deeply will ultimately lose their awe. Perhaps it's as the old adage says…

Familiarity breeds contempt.
Or more likely,
Knowledge is pain.

Although I had education in anatomy, physics, biology, chemistry, physiology, etc., I still can't shake the nagging feeling that science is like the universe; it's mostly empty space. Before you kneel at the altar of science, you might wish to consider the following:

- 900 years ago, Science refused to believe that people had circulatory systems.
- 500 years ago, Science refused to believe the world was round.
- 200 years ago, Science refused to believe that germs existed or could cause disease.
- 150 years ago, Science didn't believe in radio waves.
- 90 years ago, Science didn't believe in penicillin.
- 70 years ago, Science thought space travel was impossible.
- 50 years ago, Science scoffed at Linus Pauling's theory on Vitamin C's beneficial health effects.
- How many more centuries must pass before Science admits the existence of God?

Science has been here for a few thousand years. The universe has been here for 5 billion, according to scientific estimates. How arrogant that scientists could now know anything relevant about the universe.

Five billion minus three thousand... hmmm... the numbers over-ran my desk calculator. I'll switch to the computer. One moment, please.

Ah... here we go... the universe has been here for 4,99999,7000 years *BEFORE* science. That seems like a long time; but to God, it's just the blink of an eye.

Scientific data depends upon bulk numbers to reach accurate conclusions. We see just a sliver of the universe... yet it doesn't stop science from making huge speculation from the tiny percentage of what it sees, to explain the infinite amount it can't see.

Think of it; an infinite number of galaxies, limitless expanses of space constantly expanding for five billion years. We can only measure and study less than one ten-millionth of a zillionth of a billionth of one percent of infinity. I'd say, MATHEMATICALLY speaking, *science knows zero percent about the universe.*

If you're a bean counter or physics nut, you might take issue with my numbers but my point is; pick any numbers you wish and still the universe is really big and it has been here for a really long time. We are the *newest fleas on the oldest elephant*; how could we know where she's walking? Or Why?

I know I shouldn't be wasting your precious time with my half-baked views on galactic theory, but still, I can't help myself.

I believe there is no greater question, no larger paradigm to grapple than the origin of life. It speaks to the very core of where we came from and where we will go after we die.

If you really want to see a blank look on a scientist's face, forget the "Big Bang of Matter" conundrum because he/she will just go into the catechism about how all this matter just 'materialized" from nothingness. Just like any good preacher, scientists also know their 'scripture.'

So instead of asking about matter, ask about the space. Where did all this empty space come from? What does one have to BANG, to get empty space? Anti-space? And, while you're at it, ask why the empty space keeps getting bigger. How can a vacuum get bigger? It is impossible. Vacuums tend to shrink, not expand. So either there is one huge vacuum cleaner sucking at the bordes of the universe... or the Big Bang theory sucks even more.

Virtually every field of science ultimately bangs its head against the same enigma when it comes down to the most important queries of all. Science is a bunch of intellectual cul de sacs, each one dead-ending short of the truth, these unexplainable phenomena, which force mortal minds to speculate wildly. Much like the mule chasing a carrot on a stick, science plods, blind to all but the carrot. The mule would chase it right off a cliff; I wonder if science doesn't also plod in the wrong directions.

Now, *I am NOT AGAINST SCIENCE*; it is a wonderful tool, which has given humanity many useful things. But just as any great tool, we mistakenly rely upon it when we shouldn't. We have allowed our spiritual bodies to wither, hoping the hollow babble of science will make up for the disuse atrophy slowly occurring within our hearts and souls. To expect science to answer faith-based queries is to expect pigs to fly. It is pure folly.

One day I watched a TV show on deaths of twins. In each of five highlighted cases, the surviving twin gave an eerily similar, but documented account. Although separated by many miles, (In one case by two continents) each survivor sensed the moment they lost their twin. In one case, the woman sat bolt upright from a deep sleep, at three in the morning. She woke her husband; *"Paul... Gina just died."* An hour later, a phone call confirmed it.

Ask a scientist to explain how we can sense each other like that. No scientist can explain it.

Well, there was one; Albert Einstein tried, but we were too foolish to listen. He said if you took an atom and sent one of its electrons off into space (spinning clockwise) while sending the other one (spinning counterclockwise) in another direction... both electrons would always know about their twin electron. Furthermore, he claimed that if you reversed the spin on one, the twin would simultaneously reverse its spin. If that's not weird enough for you, Albert said that this would occur regardless of how far apart they grew... across space!

If a mere electron can do it, why not human twins? To me that is the most mathematical example of God we shall ever see; God knows the falling of a single sparrow; why not electrons? For a sentient being this would be child's play…

Creating every particle in the known galaxies, watching over an infinite number of novas, supernovas, black holes, sparrows, human souls, the heavens, the firmament… God is awesome, to the infinitely cubed power.

Why should we fear our earthly death?

CHAPTER SEVEN
SIX TYPES OF DEATH

[illegible]

CHAPTER SEVEN
SIX TYPES OF DEATH

I believe there are six types of death. Now, you can argue and quote scripture and you'll be right while I'll be wrong, but since it's my book, here goes!

There is 'never-born' death, for stillborn babies, abortions and miscarriages, where the spirit was recalled before the physical body ever drew breath. We can't know God's plan, but I believe these spirits go back to the maker to await new clay to inhabit.

There is 'walking-around' death for non-believers and coin chasers. These people are truly selfish; they criticize when they should uplift. They seek material things because they think that accumulating more toys, condos and more stuff is the whole purpose of life. These people ultimately rest in the nicest coffins. Now, there's nothing wrong with affluence, but the 'walking dead' rarely use their power to help others who are less privileged. The 'walking dead' are truly dead... It is usually futile to attempt CPR. *(Christian Prayer Resuscitation; use the term if you like.)* Give them something shiny to play with, and let them be.

There is physical death, a brief transition from this life to the next. This one we all must experience.

The last category is death everlasting, for those who deny God. I'm not a preacher, so I'll leave it to those more qualified to speak on hellfire and brimstone, but here's the short version; it's *Hell, for Dummies.*

But isn't that just FOUR types of death? Read on.

Brain dead… these people were born without a brain. They can't figure out why or how we got here. Actually, they don't even try. The Brain-Dead are two-legged hamsters on a tread wheel, robotically pushing forward, getting nowhere, until they keel over and die.

Cardiac dead… these people were born without a heart. They muddle through life without ever feeling God, feeling or giving love or helping others. It is for this type of person I feel the most sorrow when they pass away. They never really lived.

CHAPTER EIGHT
FAMOUS LAST WORDS

I don’t know what my last words shall be, but I’m sure they won't be famous. You see, so far, I have led a small life without fame.

But there were three times when I truly thought my end was at hand. In each case, strangely, I felt peace, along with empathy for those I was about to leave behind. I’ll bet that your thoughts might be similar.

I have never known a man to think of himself
when dying. Never.
Antoine De Saint-Exupery

I hope the following quotes bring some mirth or ease.

By the way, the juxtapositions are intentional. I placed Charlie Chaplin next to Buddha, and murderers next to heroes; in a book on death it seems fitting, *doesn’t it?*

At any rate, forgive me if I offend. Ah, what the heck; Time is short... *forgive everybody.*

Buddha

"And now, O priests, I take my leave of you; all the elements of being are transitory. Work out your salvation with diligence."

Charlie Chaplin

After a priest said "May the Lord have mercy on your soul"... *"Why not? After all, it belongs to him."*

Ludwig van Beethoven

Having just been given Last Rites:
"Friends applaud, the comedy is over."

George Appel

A gangster in the electric chair:
"Well, gentlemen, you're about to see a baked Appel."

Julius Caesar
Gaius Caligula, Roman Emperor, stabbed by his own guards (as reported by Tacitus):
"I am still alive!"

James French
Sentenced to death in the electric chair:
"How about this for a headline for tomorrow's paper? 'French Fries'."

Joe DiMaggio
"I'll finally get to see Marilyn."

Genghis Khan
"Let not my end disarm you, and on no account weep or keen for me, lest the enemy be warned of my death."

Jimmy Glass
Murderer, while sitting in the Louisiana electric chair:
"I'd rather be fishing."

Nathan Hale, patriot, before being executed:
"I only regret that I have but one life
to lose for my country."

Robert Alton Harris
Sitting in the gas chamber.
"You can be a king or a street sweeper,
but everyone dances with the grim reaper."

Doc Holliday: gambler, gunfighter.
"This is funny."

Jesus Christ

"It is finished." John 19:30
"My God, my God, why have you forsaken me!" Mark 15:34-5 and Matthew 27:46
"Father, into thy hands I commend my spirit." Luke 23:46

Pablo Picasso
"Drink to me!"

Otto Lilienthal, flight pioneer, dying the day after he crashed one of his gliders:
"Sacrifices must be made!"

Breaker Morant
On facing a firing squad:
"Shoot straight, you bastards!
Don't make a mess of it!"

Oscar Romero, Archbishop of El Salvador,
After being shot while administering the Eucharist.
"May God have mercy on the assassins."

CHAPTER NINE
REMARKS ABOUT GOD

You have to believe in gods to see them.
Hopi Indian saying

Your idol is shattered in the dust to prove that God's dust is greater than your idol.
Rabindranath Tagore

We always believe God is like ourselves, the indulgent think him indulgent and the stern, terrible.
Joseph Joubert

We may seek God by our intellect, but we can only find him with our heart.
Cotvos

What men usually ask for when they pray to God is, that two and two may not make four.
Russian proverb

The grace of God is a wind which is always blowing.
Sri Ramakrishna

There is no God but God.
The Koran

Men must be governed by God, or they will be ruled by tyrants.
William Penn

Nothing is void of God, his work is everywhere his full of himself.
Seneca

On Faith

In the absence of scientifically proven facts, I look to faith for my answers. I have faith in god. I also have faith that the sun is shining, even though I can't prove it. Our sunshine is 8 minutes old; it takes that long for the sun's rays to travel to Earth. So the sun could have died seven and a half minutes ago and we wouldn't know it. Still, I have faith in the sun's existence. I also believe it will shine tomorrow, but I can't prove that it will.

My faith is only based upon past experience of seeing the sun every day for 57 years. They tell me the sun has been around for billions of years before I was born... and I believe them, even though nobody can prove it. Belief is the foundation of faith.

I enter an elevator taking me to a penthouse restaurant. An unknown construction company built the elevator; and probably the lowest bidder at that. Still I have faith it won't crash, because there's a plaque on its wall that says it passed some test when I wasn't there to witness it.

The high-rise won't collapse either; I have faith that whoever built it did the job right. When I order my food, I have faith that the chef won't kill me, even though I didn't inspect the kitchen or even see the chef and her sous chefs wash their hands.

I have faith in god for the same reasons. I have read the "plaques" he left us. I believe that Jesus Christ walked the earth too, because many people told the same stories about Jesus. The world keeps time and calendars based upon Jesus' birth. Clearly, he lived. If it weren't so, I doubt he'd be so famous.

When I think of the origin of the universe, I can't help but think of God. It is impossible for me to think otherwise. Then there's the 'inspection plaque.' The Bible says God made it. There is no other valid period-based claim... so by default, God did it. How do I know this? Because both science and faith came to the same conclusion and whenever that happens, I go with God because he has the best track record.

I see God in all things. I can't help it; God proves himself in countless ways and in all forms. You'd have to be blind not to see it. I don't know how long it took God to create the universe; the Bible says six days. Were these 'days' metaphors for millennia? How would I know? The details are left out, because God doesn't micromanage.

But just as the sun could've gone supernova six minutes ago, we take these things on faith. I see no reason to apologize to anyone for my faith; neither should you.

"FAITH HEALING"

When I cut myself, I have faith it will heal because my cuts have always healed before. My faith is based upon prior experience. When my patients get the flu I know they'll heal because they have always healed in the past.

I know my patients will get well because healing is intentional and intelligent; the healthful life force expression is the purpose of life. Without this life force there would be nothing alive on Earth. I can't explain it, but then I can't explain our precarious existence on Mother Earth, either.

How did we happen to end up on the solar system's ONLY planet capable of sustaining life? Luck? Glue? Random particles, long ago, spontaneously coupling together in primordial ooze... Big Bang or Divine creation?

I believe God created the universe. I will continue to believe this until such time as science can give me a factual explanation that works better... and by factual, I mean something considerably more concrete than "Big Bang," primordial soup and spontaneous generation. To believe in the scientific explanations requires more faith than it does to just say.... 'God made it.'

Until science deals me better cards,

I'll keep playing poker with God.

Three questions are worthy of serious inspection...

Where did I come from?
Why am I here?
Where am going?

The answer to all three is... God.

My scientific, rational mind would love to complicate it, perhaps make it easier to accept by making it seem more "hi-tech" or sophisticated. It's always the rational brain that gives us the fits, isn't it?

But just as with ALL of life's power lessons, it's simple. We don't need six years of college physics to get it. That's why God kept it so simple. God wants everyone to get it... even those with cognitive challenges, delays and impairments.

The Bible opens with a simple,
strong statement about the beginning;

"In the beginning, God created
the heavens and the earth."

It's as simple as that. You can certainly complicate it, if you prefer... call it Big Bang, spontaneous generation or whatever you like, but it won't change anything.

God made the universe and everything in it, including our souls... which answers the second query; "why am I here?"... because God made you. And it answers the last one, too; when we die, we'll go back to wherever we were, before we were born...

Like I said... It's simple.

All paths lead to God...
Some just take longer

I know people who never got God until their final days. I know others who accepted Christ when they were kids... and I know a few that never did feel God; even though they spent every Sunday in church, singing hymns and saying the words and still they didn't get it.

My point is that spiritual rebirth is a matter of timing, which is unique to each person's needs. When the time is right, it happens... but when the time is wrong, no amount of church babble is going to change it.

True change comes from the heart. So it's no surprise that asking God to come into your heart is something that also must come from your heart.

If this is your time to accept Christ, you'll feel it; tell God you're sorry for your sinning. Ask forgiveness. Beg Him to enter your heart, in Jesus' name. Open a Bible. There is a kingdom in Heaven with your name on a chair. All you have to do is take it.

"If you declare with your mouth, 'Jesus is Lord,'
and believe in your heart that
God raised him from the dead,
you wil be saved."
Romans 10:9

So, before you leave this planet, be sure you know where you're going. Have a good voyage; we'll see you on the other side.

AFTER WORD

This concludes my latest look at death and dying. The first look came when I was just a boy. My mother came outside while I was watering the garden; "Stevie... did you know... Mr. B is *DEAD?"* Perhaps not the best way to inform a young boy his role model has passed, but it sure as hell was the fastest. Life on the farm is sometimes brutal, but always efficient.

He was more than a baseball coach. He was my mentor and substitute father. Every kid on the team loved him. He was so devoted to kids and baseball; he could make you feel the highest with just a grin and the lowest with a scowl. What a good man. I stood there, my tears mixing with the water; how would my world ever be the same?

Well, it wasn't the same; it was worse. The first rude awakening came during play-offs. We played a team famous for cheating, but Coach had always kept them honest. With him gone, they cheated us shamelessly, while we were still numb from his death. It taught me a harsh fact; life goes on. We lose someone, we hurt like the very hinges of Hell are burning us, we grieve and our world is never the same. And then, one day too soon, it's our turn to die and cause others that same pain and loss. And then, what happens after that? Well, opinions vary, so here's mine...

Life's short. *Pray hard.*
In Jesus' name...
Amen!

Steve Kooyers, Ukiah CA, USA, Earth, July 2010

Fin...

(or *is it?*)

www.ingramcontent.com/pod-product-compliance
Lightning Source LLC
LaVergne TN
LVHW012334100826
845148LV00017B/2562

* 9 7 8 0 9 8 2 7 0 3 1 1 3 *